PENGUIN BOOKS

CONVERTED INTO HOUSES

Charles A. Fracchia, a former stockbroker and investment banker, is now a free-lance writer whose articles often appear in *Rolling Stone, Playgirl,* and *Penthouse* magazines, the *Christian Science Monitor,* and many other periodicals. He also serves as associate editor of *Bay Area Lifestyle* (the largest regional publication devoted to singles in the country) and the *San Francisco Review of Books.* His fondness for the old extends to include a devout interest in preservation: he served for several years on the San Francisco Historical Landmarks Commission (the official board responsible for designating the landmarks in San Francisco), and he is a trustee of the California Historical Society.

Jeremiah O. Bragstad worked as an architect before turning professional photographer in 1964. His colorful work can frequently be seen in, among others, *Architectural Record, Progressive Architecture, Architectural Digest, American Home, House & Garden,* and the *Los Angeles Times.* He is a member of the American Society of Magazine Photographers and, like Charles Fracchia, resides in San Francisco.

CONVERTED INTO HOUSES

Charles A. Fracchia

Photographs by **Jeremiah O. Bragstad**

 **PENGUIN BOOKS**

Penguin Books Ltd, Harmondsworth, Middlesex, England
Penguin Books, 625 Madison Avenue, New York, New York 10022, U.S.A.
Penguin Books Australia Ltd, Ringwood, Victoria, Australia
Penguin Books Canada Ltd, 2801 John Street, Markham, Ontario, Canada L3R 1B4
Penguin Books (N.Z.) Ltd, 182-190 Wairau Road, Auckland 10, New Zealand

First published in the United States of America by The Viking Press 1976
First published in Great Britain by Thames & Hudson Ltd 1977
Published in Penguin Books 1977

ISBN 0 14 00.4512 0

Printed in Japan by Dai Nippon Printing Company, Ltd.
Set in Helvetica
Designed by Neil Stuart

Contents

Foreword

During one of the barbarian invasions of Rome, many citizens whose homes were either destroyed or confiscated created new ones for themselves in the Colosseum. Domestic use of structures originally built to function as something other than places of residence has been a recurrent factor throughout the world, throughout history. Wars, fires, floods, earthquakes, and other disasters—natural and man-created—periodically destroy the living quarters of various segments of society, often necessitating the creation of shelter within structures which were not initially conceived as homes. After all, it is far easier and considerably more economical to adapt a sequestered monastery, abandoned mill, or bankrupt brewery to serve as a home than it is to build one anew.

During the past two decades, there has been a rapidly growing interest in the old and in preserving what exists. This movement has manifested itself in many ways: the passion for collecting antiques, even for artifacts manufactured within the last quarter century; the nostalgia craze; the interest in conservation and ecology; and, of course, preservation of architecturally and historically significant buildings.

This "mania" has been one primary factor in motivating people to acquire an environmental space which had not been designed or built to function as a home. There are many other reasons for doing so. In some cases, economic concerns—the desire for inexpensive housing—is the controlling motive; in other situations, financial matters are of relatively minor concern. Indeed, frequently the cost of acquiring a building, plus the cost of conversion, could have built or purchased a palatial dwelling.

Love of the unusual, desire for interesting architectural design and solid construction, and for unconventional space to meet living—and oftentimes working—requirements are yet other considerations. In general, however, the practical and aesthetic reasons are intermingled.

Whether the delight is in the patina of age, in the whimsy of entering a room through an oversized freezer door, or in the enjoyment of the warmth of old-brick walls, the person who transforms an environment once utilized as a factory, barn, water tower, or whatever other non-dwelling use into a home is opting for an unusual living experience: a flight from the increasing conformity, artificiality, anonymous construction, and shoddy craftsmanship that afflict modern society.

This criticism of the bland living environment endemic in our world—and the attempt of an increasing number of people to escape it—is not new. Perhaps the most articulate voice of protest came from William Morris during the late nineteenth century. Witnessing the economic explosion of the Industrial Revolution—which spread loathsome slums, downed ancient trees, mass-produced furniture and artifacts of ineffable ugliness—Morris roared against such desecration and worked to bring about a revival of good taste in architecture, the decorative arts, and even typography. But even Morris's titanic figure could not halt the aesthetic rape of England.

What, then, have the owners of these recycled structures accomplished? Is it merely self-indulgence? The whims of the rich to have "funky" places to live? Since the phenomenon of converting non-dwelling structures into houses is a recent one, it is not yet possible to determine what effect this movement will have. Aside from the conversion of the occasional barn, mill, estate carriage house, or water tower in a rural or suburban area, what will happen to the great mass of buildings in urban areas: obsolete factories, old social halls, abandoned churches? Will there be wholesale destruction of these buildings—such as the Redevelopment Agency's obliteration of a large proportion of San Francisco's Victorian houses—or will urban dwellers see these buildings as opportunities to acquire what could be low-cost housing?

Cost of conversion of the houses illustrated in this book varies greatly. In some instances, the owners spared no expense: architects, contractors, decorators were fully consulted and commissioned to do the transformation. In others, the owners did the work—minimal or radical—and bought all the necessary materials themselves.

"When you buy a place like this," said one owner of a converted house who did the work by himself and with the help of some friends, "the first thing you have to do is to buy the *New York Times* book on household repairs. You begin to learn fast. Also, your friends with construction skills are eager to help you. It becomes a community project—an exercise in creativity."

Since the buildings that become converted into houses have limited use as they stand—and a limited number of people interested in acquiring them—generally they can be purchased for very little money. In fact, in most cases it appears that the building in question was "thrown in" with the acquisition of the land.

In many cases, the conversion of a building into a house is executed to provide a combination of living space and working quarters. This is particularly true for artists. A firehouse provided splendid studios as well as a residence for tapestry and stained-glass-window designer Mark Adams and his printmaker wife, Beth van Hoesen. An industrial loft fulfilled the living and working requirements of filmmaker Paul Aratow. And Marion Saltman can conduct her play therapy groups on the decks of the *Vallejo* and never leave her home. In the spirit of the medieval craftsman, illustrator Nicolas Cann can preside over his drawing tables, walk only a few feet to the comforts of his living quarters, and all within the confines of a bank building.

And lifestyles of the occupants vary considerably, from those who wish to live in lavish style to those who desire simplicity.

There can be no generalizations about those who have labored to transform a non-dwelling building into their home. Their reasons for the conversion vary. The experiences of conversion are different. Uses for these dwellings differ. What seems to be a constant is the desire for unconventional living space, and a deep-seated pride and delight in their environmental creations.

The concept for this book developed out of my association with another, *Handmade Houses: A Guide to the Woodbutcher's Art,** a photographic essay of houses and other structures built by the owners themselves. The lyrically exciting quality of the photographs of these buildings, portraying an excursion into architectural and environmental fantasy-turned-reality, analogized itself in my mind to already existing buildings which had been converted to houses: not the renovated Victorian in San Francisco or brownstone in New York, but structures which had not been built as houses or used as such.

*Scrimshaw Press. 1973.

The idea rapidly became a project. Architectural photographer Jeremiah O. Bragstad joined me as a partner. Book design and production consultant Richard Schuettge and real estate broker Susan M. Mitchell completed the quartet of those who would work on the project. Our friends were polled to discover places suitable for inclusion in the book. Countless hours were spent writing letters and on the telephone tracking down places we heard about. Some of the more unusual conversions which, for one reason or another, we could not include were: a movie studio, an aviary, a funeral parlor, a silo, a gasoline station (in which the grease pit was used as the bathtub), a mill, a mine, and a brewery. Our "discoveries"—both numerous and varied—began to astound us!

We had early decided to limit our selections to converted houses in Northern California; but the lure of places we heard about, first in Southern California, then in the East, and finally in Europe proved too tempting. We expanded the geographical scope of the book.

Long drives to out-of-the-way places, detective work in locating houses for which we had imperfect addresses, allaying the fears of nervous owners that their homes would become tourist attractions (or the target of some overzealous building inspector), and many hours spent interviewing owners about the histories of their dwellings and the process of conversion were characteristic in the gestation of this book.

In the process, we got lost many times, spent a great deal of time searching out false leads, once discovered that film for a particularly delectable photographic session had become overexposed, were run off at gun point from one piece of property—all adventures which adversely worked to increase our relish for the project.

We wish to express our most sincere appreciation and gratitude to all the owners of the converted houses which appear in this book—men and women who warmly welcomed us into their homes, patiently discussed them with us, expressed interest in what we were doing, and offered us encouragement. These men and women—who have chosen to rescue and restore, to pour their resources of time, energy, and money into the imaginative conversion of buildings into homes, and whose aim, aside from the creation of desired living spaces, was to insure the preservation of many an unusual building and thereby add to the architectural flavor of the community—we praise as environmental pioneers.

It is our hope that these men and women—and this book—will encourage others to do likewise, to create similiar imaginative designs in living.

—Charles A. Fracchia
San Francisco, California
November 10, 1975

"Intimate Confines"
A Chicken Coop

One doesn't generally consider a chicken coop as a possibility for human habitation, but Byron Randall's ownership of one, on his property in Sebastopol, California, challenged his resourcefulness and fired his imagination. He decided he would turn the chicken coop into a home.

Although chicken coops are not sturdily built, Randall's provided enough substance for a comfortable house. "The place was built in the 1930s or '40s," he reports. "Plenty of wood was used, and it was a perfect beginning for a house."

Randall and a helper did all the work of conversion over a four-year period. New foundations had to be constructed, as well as solid floors. Insulation and additional interior walls had to be added. And, since chickens obviously require no plumbing or wiring, Randall had to include these as well. But the chicken coop's original confines—and the weathered exterior—remained very much the same. It continues to resemble a chicken coop: a low-lying building, very much like a rustic ranch-style house or cabin.

The rooms are cluttered with Randall's enormous collection of books and with reminders of his diverse and exciting life. Trees and shrubs surround the chicken coop, lending much charm to its rusticity.

One cannot help asking why Randall went to so much trouble to convert the abandoned chicken coop. "It was absurd not to make use of what was there," he responds. "If I had had to build a place new, I would have had to do even more work. Instead, with the chicken coop, I had only to add to an existing structure."

And, yes, Randall will smilingly admit, "I get up with the chickens."

From a Shelter of Animals . . .
The Barn in the West

The western part of the United States had a much later—and much different—agricultural development than the East. For one thing, farms we larger. For another, the mild weather did not necessitate well-built structu for storing produce or housing animals. As a result, the barn, as an architectural aspect of the West, is not as important a structure as it is in East.

Barns converted into houses are a rarity in the West, which is why the discovery of a barn-house in Northern California is such a delightful experience. Located near the seacoast, this barn is more than one hundre years old. It was purchased and converted by a woman artist.

The original stalls for horses on the ground floor were torn down, and the was remodeled to accommodate a kitchen, reminiscent of a scene from a Dutch painting, dining area, and living room. An appended lean-to, which originally a tool shed, is now a small sitting room.

The second floor, which has become a bedroom and weaving studio, was originally a hayloft. In order to brighten up the interior, the owner added a skylight.

A decision to keep the exterior of the barn in its original condition and to r the interior wood siding gives this barn-house a weathered look—both ins and out—which aesthetically contrasts with the rich fabrics, colors, and objects in profusion. For its artist owner, this converted barn represents convenient living within the context of the rich patina of old wood.

The Barn in the East

There are very few buildings that can be taken apart, moved a considerable distance from their original site, and assembled once again. But this is exactly what John Millville did to a barn which had already passed its hundredth year of existence. The principal reason he was able to do so was that nails were not used in the construction of the traditional New England barn: the wood was joined together by oak pegs, which were pulled out and then inserted again.

Millville's reassembly of the barn was but the first step in his program to convert the building into a home. The interior was subject to extensive remodeling—virtually a total transformation. One now enters a large, two-story living room with a lovely cathedral ceiling. A dining room, family room, bedroom, and bathroom are also on the first floor, and an additional bedroom is upstairs.

During Millville's removal-and-conversion program, the external siding was the only section of the structure to suffer a casualty. It was replaced, however, with compatible weathered wood, so the exterior of his new home looks precisely as it did when the building fulfilled its original role.

From a Shelter of Vehicles . . .
A Mews House

It is unlikely that the former proprietors of stately mansions ever gave much thought to the small structures to the rear of their homes, which faced upon common courtyards and housed their carriages and horses. Today, these once humble structures—facing on mews and therefore called mews houses—are among the most fashionable living quarters in London and New York.

The Eglon Mews House in London was once a typical carriage house and stable, then servants' quarters, and has now been converted by its owners, Ian Haywood and Guri Halberg, into a residence of their own.

The original structure contained two stories and a hayloft. It is now a three-story house: the first floor consists of a garage, bathroom, and studio; the second holds two bedrooms, a kitchen, and a dining room; and a living room and enclosed deck occupy the third.

Haywood and Halberg did virtually all the work of conversion themselves, hiring professional builders only for the heavy construction work. All in all, the project took ten years to complete.

A Carriage House

Mirroring the change in transportation modes, a 1900 carriage house built for an estate in Taconic, Connecticut, soon became a garage for the proprietor's automobiles. And, reflecting the decline of large estates, several years ago filmmaker Bill Muyskens purchased the carriage house/garage to turn into a residence for himself.

The Norman–French-style carriage house was eminently suited to conversion into a small but elegant house. The addition of a fireplace, a few walls to create a bedroom, and necessary wiring and plumbing for housing amenities were the basic aspects of conversion, though Muyskens also altered the interior appearance of the building by adding a balcony which provided study and work space.

Despite these changes, the interior of the building remains reminiscent of its original use. The distinctive wood of the ceiling and portions of the walls convey the flavor of the times when horses drew carriages inside, and, later, when horseless carriages parked here.

Snorting Horses, Steaming Engines
A Firehouse

When the famous tapestry and stained-glass designer Mark Adams and his printmaker wife, Beth van Hoesen, appeared in a San Francisco court to bid on a piece of property that the city no longer wanted, they were surprised and appalled to see the courtroom filled with bidders: they hadn't expected so many would want the abandoned turn-of-the-century firehouse which they already envisioned as their combined home and studio. But their relief was great when they realized they were the only bidders on the firehouse; the others were speculators interested in other property. The year was 1959, and the couple spent the ensuing year in transforming the late-Victorian-style firehouse. The present studio was formerly the engine room and stable for the horses. It continues to display most of the accouterments from the days when the large doors would open and snorting horses would rush out, pulling the steaming fire engine behind them. One of the two original fire poles remains, as well as the bells which summoned firemen and horses to duty, and the "gang" shower—a common shower room for the firemen to wash away the grime and soot acquired in the line of duty.

The entrance to the firehouse is situated on one side of the building and opens onto a flight of stairs leading directly to the living quarters—a living room, kitchen and dining area, a bedroom, and a deck—thus bypassing the couple's studio on the ground floor.

Adams and Van Hoesen kept the space in their studio and home as open as possible, and their aim—to retain the simplicity of the original building wherever possible—was successfully executed.

Two Oast Houses Join

Ted and Leonora Draper recognized a pair of oast houses in Kent, England, for what they were: circular buildings for roasting hops. They also found the unusually shaped mid-nineteenth-century structures enchanting, and during the late 1960s decided to purchase them for their permanent dwelling place.

The Wickhurst Oast, as their acquisition was entitled, is an example of total conversion: five years of labor went into its charming transformation. When the building was bought, there was little else than two brick towers with conical shingled roofs. Between the two, the Drapers added a connecting middle section, which provided an entrance into the house and accommodated a staircase leading to the second floor. Rooms had to be constructed in the two towers as well. The bottom floor of one tower now holds a kitchen, bathroom, and utility room; the bottom floor of the other is now a round living room. On the top floor, one of the towers contains a bedroom, bathroom, and studio; and the other, two bedrooms and a bathroom.

The converted oast house very much resembles a medieval keep with its conical shape. But the once forbidding exterior was much lightened by the addition of windows, and the interior two floors have grace and a sense of modernity.

"It was an exciting project," recalls Ted Draper. "I'm relieved it's over, but not a day goes by when I'm not thankful that we did it."

Two Oast Houses Join

The Churning of Butter
A Creamery

The lovely town of Bodega is situated in some of California's most picturesque countryside: soft-rolling hills and green valleys. Its first settlers engaged in agriculture and dairy farming, a tradition which was to last well into the twentieth century. When Bill and Wopo Morehouse, both well-known artists from San Francisco, drove to see friends in Bodega, an hour away, they came across a "For Sale" sign on a recently abandoned creamery. They immediately knew that this was going to be their new home and studio.

The Bodega creamery was priced at an attractively low figure. Once the Morehouses bought it, they began to make it habitable—a process which is continuing. Bill Morehouse's skills in carpentry, electrical wiring, and plumbing came in handy during the long, slow process of rehabilitating the buildings. The large room one enters in the main building was translated into the living room. An intimate grouping of furniture, Bill's sculptures, and a profusion of plants give the immense room a sense of human scale. At one end of this room are large freezer doors leading to rooms in which milk and cheese were once refrigerated. The largest of these rooms now serves as a kitchen and dining area—equipped with what are today considered antiques but what a few decades ago were standard kitchen oak furnishings.

An immense area off the living room—once the creamery's processing center—is Bill Morehouse's studio. Adjoining his workroom is his wife's, in which she designs and prints lithographs and teaches printmaking to her students.

Despite the thousands of square feet in the creamery, there is not a surplus of rooms. A small room on the first floor serves as a guest bedroom. Two other bedrooms, originally the creamery's offices, are located up a flight of stairs from the main floor. The clever use of plants and Victorian furniture gives the large, stark bedrooms a sense of comfort and proportion, rather than an aura of cavernous space.

The Morehouses have retained many of the distinctive accouterments of their creamery: large overhead fans, the paymaster's cubicle from which workers were handed their daily wages through a small window, the massive doors which led into the large rooms and freezers.

Insulated Storage
An Icehouse

Paul Segal, A.I.A., relished the commission he received to transform
an unusual building in New Canaan, Connecticut, into a home for its
owner. The spare, austerely designed building was an icehouse,
built in 1900 for the storage of pond ice through the summer.
The building was well insulated with sawdust-filled walls—a factor
which makes the house very efficient in energy use, requiring no
cooling in summer and little heating in winter.
The icehouse is quite compact: each floor measured only 13′ × 15′.
Segal extended the upper level to provide additional floor space by
installing a protruding bay window, which also allows more light to
enter. Other construction work included utility connections and the
addition of a kitchenette and bathroom. The circular stairway, used
for its compactness, is painted bright yellow and acts as a constant
element visible from any portion of the house.

A Water Tower

Russian Hill is considered one of San Francisco's most attractive residential areas. Its quaint streets are lined with small Victorian cottages, elegant townhouses, and soaring luxury apartment buildings, most of them built in the 1920s.
High atop one of these apartment buildings stands a water tower, which once served the building and which has now been converted into one of the most distinctive penthouses in the United States. The view from this eminence is a sweeping one of the entire San Francisco Bay Area, from the majestic Golden Gate Bridge to the green hills which roll down to the eastern shores of the bay.

The idea for the conversion came from Henry Prien, the building's owner, who himself lived in the completed penthouse for a short time while still a bachelor. "One day I was on the roof of the building, admiring the view," he recalls, "and I looked at the water tower and thought that it could be turned into a splendid penthouse unit." Prien's basic problem was to make a livable unit out of the small space confined within the thick concrete walls of the tower. For inspiration in adopting space-saving devices, he was to turn to the shipbuilder's trade. Result: a finished apartment that very much resembles a ship's cabin.
An expanded, elegant terrace surrounds the tower, where Prien's current tenant and guests can sit, admire the view, or dine al fresco, provided the San Francisco fog does not swirl about. A short flight of stairs leads into a glass-enclosed porch, which serves as a comfortable living-room area.
From this rectangular porch one steps into the water tower itself—a small but high room which serves as a combination living room, study, and dining area. Above, built as a mezzanine, are the sleeping quarters. Off the bottom portion is a kitchen, constructed with all the compactness of a ship's galley.
The small size of the penthouse is made to seem larger by the use of sliding doors and the absence of partitions. In addition, closets, drawers, and other storage space have been built in. All in all, one has the feeling of a womblike, compact living space with extension of space provided by the sweeping panoramic view.

A Water Tower

Illustrative of an Energetic Past
A Powerhouse

A late-nineteenth-century powerhouse, built on the site of an old iron factory in Taconic, Connecticut, seems an odd building to transform into a place to live. But John Pogue's purchase sparked a reconstruction which was to yield the most fascinating residence in the area.

When Pogue bought the property in 1968, the building had already been converted into two apartments. But the construction had been poorly executed, and Pogue had to begin anew. The space in the medieval-appearing building was utilized to create a giant hall for a living and dining area (with a kitchen and bathroom at one end). A spiral staircase leads to a mezzanine which holds Pogue's bedroom.

The architectural flamboyance of this powerhouse is perhaps atypical of what one would expect in a powerhouse. The gothic exterior, however, is symbolic of the United States' skyrocketing prosperity during the latter part of the 1880s—a prosperity that provided John Pogue with an exquisite dwelling.

An Armorer's Workshop

The Marais district of Paris encompasses some of the oldest buildings in that fabled city, though few have undergone as dramatic a transformation as the current home of Jerome Ducrot. This late-sixteenth-century building, originally the workshop of an armorer, is tucked away off a narrow street and reminds one of the Paris of *The Hunchback of Notre Dame* or *The Three Musketeers*.

Changes in the interior have been extensive. The first floor of the building now contains a kitchen and a dining area, Ducrot's studio, office, and photographic darkrooms, and a splendid spiral staircase leading to the second. This second level supports a master bedroom and two other bedrooms, all of which face onto the opening that overlooks Ducrot's studio.

The result is one which the armorer who worked in this space four centuries ago would find bewildering. Although Ducrot has attempted to give the contemporaneity of his home and studio a tangible feeling of the past, the wall-less interior, the modern furniture, and the clever use of diagonal boards with spaces in between to form the second floor maximize the contrast between the building's present and past functions.

40

An Armorer's Workshop

A Doll Factory

The Soho district in New York needs little introduction. A former factory area in lower Manhattan, Soho is now recognized as New York's artistic community, as Greenwich Village once was. Sculptress Hannah Wilkie obtained loft space in one of Soho's buildings—a former doll factory—which is more than one hundred years old. Working with architect Tod Williams, who suggested a trade of his architectural and design services for her sculptures, Ms. Wilkie wished to keep the integrity of the loft space, yet make a triple division: as large a studio as possible, a separate living area, and an exhibit area for her sculpture.

One portion of the loft was designed as intimately as a doll's house, complete with low (7′ 6″) ceilings, and contains a bedroom, kitchen, bathroom, and laundry room with closets. "It was important that I get away from the mess in my studio, and I felt that the best way to do this was to construct something miniature and precise as a contrast," explains Ms. Wilkie. The exhibit area also serves as the center of her entertaining.

Designed by Williams, the construction was supervised entirely by Ms. Wilkie. She was quite open about the costs involved: "I stopped counting after $13,000, but the total cost in labor and materials was around $18,000."

44

An Industrial Building in Paris

To those who know the Paris of broad, tree-lined boulevards, the welter of tiny, twisting streets—spared during the city's transformation under Napoleon III—are not familiar. On one of these streets, so reminiscent of an earlier Paris, is a three-story steel-frame industrial building constructed in the 1930s. The first floor of this building has been converted into a home, which exists in odd contrast to the practical look and function of the structure.

The standard kitchen, dining room, and bedroom have been added, as well as a design studio adjacent to the living quarters. One of the unusual features of this conversion is the utilization of space which was—and is—a light well for a small garden. A glass window looks out onto it from the master bedroom.

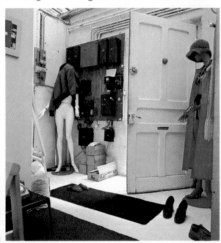

An Industrial Building in San Francisco

Industrial loft areas have long been recognized as ideal living and working places for artists of all concentrations. In the United States, they have substituted for the garrets and ateliers of Paris. Low rent, abundant space, and access to a plentitude of light are what make such areas especially desirable.

Paul Aratow rented his loft in the San Francisco Bay Area industrial town of Emeryville in 1968. The filmmaker pays $250 a month for his 4500 square feet of space, which provides him with both a studio and an apartment. Painted a stark white throughout, Aratow's loft is severely divided between its working area (decorated with huge color advertising posters of old movies) and its living quarters. The vast living area evokes warmth and comfort, accomplished primarily by the prolific distribution of plants and fascinating objects gathered during European travels. A Greek Coca-Cola sign, old cameras, an old Victrola, a pinball machine, and a small winepress are but a few of the items which enrich the space of Aratow's enormous apartment.

The Aratow loft is an example of conversion without extensive remodeling or expenditure of much money. The space was left as it was. Partitions were created, as needed, by the judicious arrangement of furniture. The floors were sanded and stained, and the walls were painted. The rest was a matter of decoration, not construction. The result: a funky, attractive home and office.

A Cannery

A West Coast photographer pays a modest monthly rent of $80 for his work studio and apartment: 2300 square feet of what was once the top floor of the Monterey Canning Company's cannery on Cannery Row, celebrated by John Steinbeck. With the exception of a small dining and kitchen area and a darkroom, the rest of the loft is left open. Atop the darkroom ceiling is the bedroom—an open space overlooking the sizable main area and reached by means of a ladder. The space is furnished and decorated quite sparsely, augmenting the feeling of gigantic openness. A grouping of pillows and couches forms a living-room section. The display of photographs provides the only other decorative break in the cavernlike room.

The occupant complains of only two matters: keeping it heated and keeping it clean. However, this is more than made up for, he says, by the convenience of being able to display his photographs to great advantage and occasionally to invite as many as three hundred guests for a party.

Spaciousness Accentuated by Lingering Odors
A Leather and Spices Factory

It seems that the French delight in contrasting exterior drabness with interior elegance in their conversion of buildings into homes. When French photographer Jean-Claude DeWolf purchased a Parisian factory building erected in 1910, he did nothing to change the dull industrial exterior but spent two years gutting and rebuilding the two interior floors. Vast skylights admit a great deal of light into DeWolf's home and photographic studio. The skylights are probably the only relics of this former leather and spices factory—the combined smells of which are still hinted in the building. Once one is inside, amid the billiard table and contemporary art, only the high ceilings and massive size of the rooms convey its former function.

A Butterscotch Factory

Fortunately, well-known London industrial designer Michael Wolff loves butterscotch. For when he decided to convert the top floor of the old Callard and Bowser's butterscotch factory—a building constructed around 1800 near Paddington Station—the many years of manufacturing had instilled the aroma of the famous butterscotch throughout the building. "The smell of butterscotch had permeated the timbers," Wolff recalls. The thick fragrance was not even eradicated during World War II, when the building served as a dormitory for air raid wardens.

Wolff looked beyond the vast, cavernous spaces inside the building, beyond the heavy late-Victorian factory exterior, and even beyond the seemingly permanent impregnation of the smell of butterscotch. He saw, instead, the possibility of converting this space into an unusual open living environment.

The top floor of the factory was refurbished, but no construction was necessary. Wolff put his considerable design talents to use and developed a casual living arrangement based on groupings of furniture—all set on casters for easy mobility and rearrangement. The result is one vast room brought into proportion by Wolff's large, but comfortable, furniture designs. A smaller space on the floor below contains the kitchen, dining room, and bathroom.

A Cigar Factory

Architect Tim Wilson created a most unusual home for himself on the top floor of one of New York's most handsome late-nineteenth-century industrial buildings—a former cigar factory. In order to eradicate the effects of its erstwhile use, Wilson had to work vigorously; for example, the floor needed five coats of paint in order to remove the tobacco stains. The loft was blessed with a large skylight, under which Wilson placed the major seating area. Plants hanging from the skylight, together with potted trees and flowers, make this living area a kind of romantic garden near the center of the open floor, which is undivided except for the kitchen and bathroom. A sleeping loft is suspended over one section.

Wilson has retained certain aspects of the building which indicate its nineteenth-century use: a potbellied stove is both decorative and practical, providing most of the heat for the loft; an antique shower is still used; and, of course, the skylight.

One of the especially pleasant attractions of Wilson's top-floor loft is his access to the roof, which is frequently used for parties.

A Cigar Factory

Awakening to an Aroma *Délicieux*
A Bakery

Who can resist the smell of freshly baked bread or pastries? Daniel Budin, a set designer for French television, maintains that he can awaken in the early morning to the smell of baked goods in the boulangerie-pâtisserie that he purchased and converted.

Aside from the alleged aroma, there is very little else that is reminiscent of the building's original use, for Budin has transformed the 1890s structure into one of the most elegant residences in Paris.

The original building had a retail shop in front, followed by the bakery, and an oven in the back of the building. The retail store, where bread and pastries were sold, is now Budin's studio; the bakery is a living room, and the space which accommodated the oven has been converted into the kitchen and dining area. A spiral staircase leads to the second floor and three bedrooms.

The Quaffing of Beer, the Singing of Songs
A German Athletic Club

Very few buildings in San Francisco predate the 1906 earthquake and fire. One of the most unusual of the surviving structures is a turnverein, or German athletic club, built in 1886. Legend states that Sarah Bernhardt performed on the stage here, but research has not verified this. What is known is that the German community of San Francisco used the building well into the twentieth century as a meeting and social hall, as an entertainment spot, and as a gathering place for the quaffing of beer in a beer garden.
The building was abandoned when David Winfield Willson and Fred Campbell purchased it several years ago and began to pour their considerable energies into converting it into a home.

The large hall became the living room. The enormous space was tamed by means of a defined assemblage of couches and other furniture. The rest of the space became a place to situate sculpture and unnecessary, but decorative, furniture. The hall's stage was supplied with lights, tied to the sound of music from the stereo. As a result, the light dances to the music in a subdued way.
A beautiful dining area and a kitchen designed to serve the semiprofessional cooking requirements of Campbell and Willson are located at the end of the hall opposite the stage. The owners extended a small balcony above the current kitchen/dining area: this is where Campbell plies his hair-styling trade. In addition, this mezzanine, where the offices for the building used to be, supports two bedrooms, an exquisite bathroom, and a large dressing room. The only other change they made was to add a wooden deck.
Campbell and Willson point out that there is still a great deal of space in the building which they've yet to tackle: the rooms above the stage; an entire ground floor; and large freezers situated against one of the outer walls of the building, which they contemplate turning into a sauna.

With Wood to Spare
A Lumberyard

Stefan Novak, like many who live in structures which were not originally built as houses, is an artist. His massive sculptures grace many parks and building plazas throughout the West.

It was natural that a lumberyard in Berkeley, California, should have attracted his attention when he and his wife were looking for suitable housing several years ago. The lumberyard, up for sale, had the advantage of being able to serve both as home and work area: the company's office building, an undistinguished two-story rectangular structure, would provide the Novaks with a home; the huge lumber shed behind the building would become his studio.

Novak's expertise in building skills served him well. While the lumber shed needed no transformation to suit his purpose, and the exterior of the office building would remain substantially the same, the interior needed extensive construction work and was completely transformed to Novak's taste. The first floor now consists of a large living room, a small, compact study, a kitchen, and a bathroom. The second floor, constructed as a mezzanine, holds three bedrooms, a bathroom, and a utility room for storage and laundry.

Novak designed the kitchen so that it can be utilized with a minimum of moving about. One exceptional example of his ability to design and construct a usable room from odd space is the study situated beneath the staircase leading to the second floor. As a result of his compact carpentry, Novak has fashioned the space into a multi-drawer and desk area.

Other changes, including the construction of a large stone fireplace, the elimination of some walls, and the addition of large glass windows facing the back yard and the shed, give this former office building a warm, light, and airy ambience.

A Lumberyard

A Lumberyard

Floating Homes, Floating Workshops
A Tugboat

When William Harlan decided to buy an old tugboat, he also decided that he would spare nothing in transforming it into a well-designed floating home. Docked among the boats of Sausalito's famous houseboat community, the transformed dwelling is now rented to sea-loving actor Sterling Hayden. Marine architecture—which stresses functional use of every available space—dictated the conversion of Harlan's tugboat. A tile-and-redwood sauna, which doubles as a bathtub, is tucked away in a niche of the boat; mirrors over the bed and at the headboard give the illusion of a much larger sleeping area; and the construction of a bathroom in the old bridge or wheelhouse is yet another example of practical and aesthetic expansion of compact space.

The living room is filled with Hayden's furniture and memorabilia collected over many years of world travel. It is the only area on the tugboat which allows for a certain amount of decorative flexibility, but it still retains much of the original tugboat's roughhewn decor.

A Ferry Boat

Before the five bridges that now cross various parts of San Francisco Bay were built, ferry boats crisscrossed the bay, transporting passengers and freight—and later automobiles—to and from the various communities that hug the extensive shoreline of this beautiful bay.

The construction of the bridges, beginning in the 1930s, spelled the end of the white leviathans. One after another they were withdrawn from service and often destroyed, until the ferry service was finally discontinued in the mid-1950s. (It is significant that the Golden Gate Bridge Authority has once more inaugurated the use of commuter ferries from San Francisco to Marin County in order to ease automobile traffic on the bridge.)

One bay ferry that escaped deterioration and dismantlement is the S.S. *Vallejo.* Built in 1879, it went back and forth between Vallejo (at the mouth of the Sacramento River), Mare Island (the venerable naval base), and San Francisco until it was retired in 1948.

The huge ferry was purchased by artist Gordon Onslow-Ford for use as his home and studio. Beached at Waldo Point, a marshy area in colorful Sausalito, it looked out to Mount Tamalpais over quiet waters troubled only by seagulls, grebes, wild ducks, terns, and pelicans. Onslow-Ford completed some minimal construction to divide the ferry boat lengthwise and invited his friend and fellow artist, the ebullient bohemian Jean Varda, to live and work in one half.

Eventually, Onslow-Ford moved out, and his half of the stately ferry was occupied by philosopher Alan Watts. Since Watts' death, the space has become the headquarters for The Alan Watts Society for Comparative Philosophy. And, since the death of Jean Varda, his half has been occupied by play therapist Marion Saltman.

The distinguished lineage of the S.S. *Vallejo* gives the venerable ship the aspect of a shrine. The half of the ship where Varda—friend of Henry Miller, Anais Nin, and other artists who settled on the West Coast—lived, painted, and cavorted with the young women who flocked about him, continues to show his artistry. The tops of the pier posts to which the *Vallejo* is secured are decorated with multicolored faces. The furniture and decorations of the interior are as he left them; they display his imaginative use of odd pieces of wood, junk, and nature's droppings such as driftwood, rocks, and shells to create an environment of fantasy and color.

Its current use by Marion Saltman for her living quarters and groups in play therapy very much identifies with its lighthearted, whimsical design.

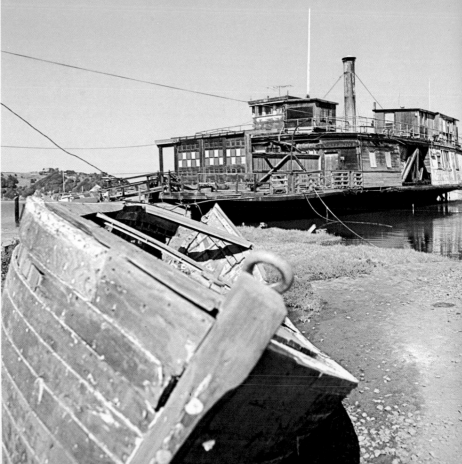

A Ferry Boat

The mood changes when one walks through a door into the area which houses Watts' Society for Comparative Philosophy. A hushed quiet pervades these austere quarters. The rooms are larger. The decor is stark white and black: the simplicity of the Orient. Watts' executor lives here, promoting the philosopher's work in making Eastern ideas known to the West.

The S.S. *Vallejo* dominates the waterside in Sausalito, where every conceivable type of water dwelling is moored. Its fame is known throughout the area. No one who visits this ferry boat—its exterior virtually unchanged from its days of plying the waters of San Francisco Bay—leaves without being charged with its historical role, its sense of fun, and the intimate presence of its "ghosts."

Three Barges

Europe's ample waterways have long been the traditional arteries of transportation. In England and on the continent, barges, whose basic construction has not changed for centuries, carried coal, grain, and fodder.

Three such barges—now river-based homes for their owners—are located in the Paris area. *La Linquenda*—eating area (top right), former captain's cabin (center right), and pilot house (bottom left)—is anchored near the Tuileries. *L'Arche de Noé,* of which we see only the exterior, rests near Louveciennes; *L'Ardea* (bottom right and opposite) serves both as a home for owner Philip Rouff and as a craft for tours of French and German rivers.

The latter barge, which was built in England in the 1920s, carried coal and grain on the Norfolk and Suffolk waterways for many years before Rouff's purchase and its transformation into a floating home and place of work. Its conversion is impressive when one considers that the boat was constructed entirely out of teak—a wood extremely difficult to work.

Railroad Living of Style
A Caboose

Elsie Fraser and Helen Walters hadn't planned on buying anything when they went poking around a salvage yard several years ago. But when they came across two train cabooses, built by the Pullman Car Company in 1916 for the Western Pacific Railroad, now abandoned and for sale at a very low price, they instantly decided that they must have them.

As they had them hauled two hundred miles to the community of Little River, near Mendocino, California, they didn't realize that their decision to convert one of the cabooses into their residence and the other (not shown) into a gift shop would occupy all their weekends and vacation time for the next five years. One of their first tasks was to construct a passageway from one caboose to the other. Although the distinctive features and flavor of the original cabooses were kept, the two women were involved in making compact spaces designed for travel both comfortable and convenient for year-round living. In their new home, bathroom and kitchen facilities had to be expanded, and windows had to be enlarged. A bedroom and living room take up the remaining space.

A Pullman Car

During the plastic and conforming decade of the 1950s, two men—the late Lucius Beebe and Charles Clegg—reached back to the nineteenth century for models of elegance, style, and nonconformity. Railroads held a fascination for both, and they purchased an abandoned Pullman car from the Great Northern Railroad in 1955. The massive sleeping car (weighing more than ninety tons, with inside dimensions of 86 feet by 9½ feet) had run on the Oriental Limited. The train, whose route extended between Chicago and the West Coast, was de-commissioned by the railroad during the 1940s.

Beebe and Clegg brought it to a private siding in Reno, Nevada, where they converted it into a traveling dwelling. When it was completed, it was the only private railroad car in the country.

The conversion demolished four ladies' dressing rooms to construct the present galley or kitchen area. Next to it is the lovely dining room. Two bedrooms, with a bathroom, are situated in the middle of the car. Clegg is proud of the fact that this railroad car was the first to employ chemical toilets.

An elegant drawing room—replete with fireplace—completes the railroad car, with the exception of a charming vestibule which serves as the entry chamber.

"The Virginia City," as the car is christened, is decorated in the flamboyant style of the nineteenth century: A Venetian baroque decorative style reminiscent of the railroad palaces of the robber barons. Says Clegg, "We designed the car to capture the elegance of the Palace of the Doges in Venice."

The conversion of the railroad car from a Pullman sleeper to the compact house that it is today did not change its solid steel exterior, which is now painted the Amtrak colors.

A Railroad Station in the West

From the early nineteenth century until recent years, the spreading network of railroads provided an essential lifeline in the transportation of persons and goods to a rapidly growing United States. With the advent of the automobile and the truck, and with the profound economic and social changes which transformed the face of the nation following World War II, the railroad lost much of its importance. Many lines were abandoned, and the railroad stations that dotted every town along the locomotive's path became obsolete.

One such station, in the town of Capitola (near Santa Cruz, California), was built in 1901 by the Southern Pacific Railroad to serve this small community. By mid-century it became obvious that the area could no longer support a railroad stop. In 1958 Southern Pacific sold the Capitola railroad station to one of its officials for the piddling fee of one dollar.

In 1971 it was sold again. The new owner also paid one dollar, but, unlike his predecessor who had not made any use of his holding, he converted his 1000-square-foot depot into a charming home.

The original clapboard—a tribute to the stinginess of Collis P. Huntington, one of the "Big Four" who founded the railroad—was shingled. The depot's thirteen-foot-ceilinged waiting room was converted into the present living room, and the workroom into the kitchen and dining room. The freight room, in which railroad employees once wrestled with packages, is used as a master bedroom; and the station's toolroom, connected with the main building but reached only from outside the depot, has been transformed into a guest bedroom.

Most of the characteristic railroad-station features have nonetheless remained: the bay window of the present dining room is where train tickets were once sold; the central pane still sports the protruding customer ledge; and the front windows and the massive 8′ × 4′ door have survived as they were.

The expanse of land surrounding the station affords the owners privacy and quiet. Part of the front property is a public park, and the owners have installed a small, shallow pool in the rear.

The train continues to pass by the depot twice a day, and though it has not stopped for over twenty years, its light waves a traditional signal on passing—a remembrance of when the building served as a regular stop for the railroad.

84

A Railroad Station in the East

The nostalgic lore of American railroads continues to fire the imagination of buffs throughout the country. Despite the fact that the railroad is rapidly disappearing from the landscape, an increasing number of enthusiasts collect and enjoy all the paraphernalia of railroading. Consequently, it is not surprising that abandoned railroad stations should be desired for homes or offices. One such station, built in 1870 during the golden age of railroads, is in Sheffield, Massachusetts. During the latter part of the nineteenth century, when financial titans such as Gould, Morgan, and Vanderbilt endlessly struggled for control of Eastern and Midwestern railroads, the community of Sheffield was served by this picturesque station.

When Sheffield ceased to be a stop for the railroad, the station was abandoned and sold for $1000. The owners moved the building four miles to its present site and converted it into a home, retaining virtually all the distinctive features of its railroad-station style—the original façade of the building, including the station windows, the imposing height of the ceilings, and the octagonally contoured men's and women's toilets. The original ticket office, also octagonal in shape, is the current kitchen.

The year 1923 was a prosperous one in the United States. The post–World War I recession was over, business was booming, and a feeling of perennial affluence pervaded the country. It was in this year that a group of Los Angeles businessmen founded a bank in Palms, California, near the MGM studio. Apparently, they had assumed that the booming movie business would bring vast deposits for their banking venture.

But seven years later the euphoria ended: the stock market crashed, and the country was in the grip of the worst depression in its history. The bank in Palms failed, and its classic Renaissance exterior—evocative of banking solidity and stability—soon became an unusual façade for an unemployment office, a post office, and a furniture warehouse in turn.

In 1970 illustrator Nicolas Cann bought the building and moved in without delay. Despite forty years of vicissitudes, the bank building was still in its original condition when Cann purchased it. But it required a great deal of interior reconstruction, all of which progressed under the watchful eye of Cann, who lived there throughout the transition from bank to living and working quarters. "It wasn't an easy task," Cann recalls. "It was a year before I even had hot water."

Cann sought flexibility in his renovation and achieved this by incorporating additions which were capable of easy dismantlement; thus all the new construction was attached by means of large screws.

88

One enters Cann's residence through the original doors of the bank, then walks into a small entry area separated from the rest of the floor by a screen. Behind the screen is the high-ceilinged former banking floor, which is now Cann's "entertaining" space. Here he can visit with a handful of friends or serve a dinner for two hundred and fifty guests. Bookcases cover one entire wall. Another screen separates this room from the rear half of the bank. Along one side of this section are Cann's drawing tables, and in the back is the kitchen. A loft and a small second floor provide a bedroom and a guest bedroom. Beneath the loft is a small dining area.

Like others who have converted massive spaces into comfortable living quarters, Cann has managed to take what appears to be unwieldy space and, by application of imagination and creative design, utilize the space for effective living and working areas.

Where Once the School Bells Tolled
A Schoolhouse

John Ward, a California real estate developer, had always admired the picturesque nineteenth-century schoolhouse located on the Montezuma Slough, near the delta area where the Sacramento and San Joaquin rivers join and flow into San Francisco Bay.

To Ward, the schoolhouse represented a forgotten aspect of California history: the river transportation of the state's abundant agricultural products. When the quaint schoolhouse was no longer used, Ward bought it and renamed the site where it stood "Ward's Landing."

Little had to be done in the way of converting the schoolhouse into a home. The principal's office, where, no doubt, many a misbehaved child felt the lash of a ruler, is now Ward's bedroom. The two lavatories—still marked "Girls" and "Boys"—are his children's bedrooms. And the large room where children of all ages studied reading, writing, and arithmetic now contains a kitchen (separated from the rest of the room by a counter) and the living room and dining area.

A few feet from the old schoolhouse, Ward has placed two old barges—both almost two hundred feet long—which remind Ward of that glorious chapter in California's economic history.

Another Schoolhouse

In 1873 Bodega, California, was a bustling lumber town. When members of the community decided that it was time to build a schoolhouse, they constructed a large, two-story frame building, giving it a flourish by adding a cupola to the top. Today, Bodega is a tiny hamlet in the midst of a huge agricultural area to the north of San Francisco, but the schoolhouse still stands on a knoll overlooking the town—even though children no longer respond to the clang of a bell announcing that class is about to begin.

The schoolhouse was abandoned when gallery owner Tom Taylor purchased it several years ago. He found it ideal for both his art gallery and his home, and proceeded to install his exhibits on the ground floor, retaining the flavor of the original large classroom. The fixtures, stoves, and even a few desks are as they were when the building was still an institution of learning.

The second floor was transformed into living quarters, using the same expedient by which the bottom was converted into an art gallery: redecoration. Taylor decided against dividing the huge space of the second floor into smaller rooms. Thus, the dining area, sleeping quarters, and living room are distinguished by a judicious arrangement of furniture. The spacious room was made warmer, more intimate, by the use of lush rugs on the floor and paintings and tapestries on the walls. An existing bathroom had to be remodeled and a small kitchen added for cooking facilities—but that was all.

A House of People
A Church

When changing neighborhood patterns instigated the construction of a new Saint Aidan's Episcopal Church in another section of San Francisco, the late-nineteenth-century church was put up for sale. Though the old church commanded an excellent view of both the city and the bay, no one seemed to want this rustic edifice, primarily because the upper Haight-Ashbury district, where the church is located, seemed to be "in the hands of hippies." As a consequence, the purchase price was quite low. In 1965 Ms. Bonnie Koven, on the staff of the San Francisco Museum of Art, bought the building, and she was to expend $22,000 in renovations in creating a new home for herself and her children.

As one enters the former vestibule (now the entry hall), one immediately senses a spirit of quiet: it is difficult to speak except in hushed tones. A short corridor leads to a bedroom, which was the only new room constructed in the nave of the former church. The same corridor steers into the main area, where once congregations sat to listen to the Word of the Lord, and which is now a combined living room, playroom, and study.

A huge stone fireplace was installed where the altar stood. Subdued light enters from stained-glass windows. At one end, over the bedroom on the main floor (in what was the choir loft), is another bedroom.

Behind the large fireplace, in what was once the sacristy, where ministers would vest for services, is a large modern kitchen and dining area.

Although Ms. Koven's reconstruction does not seem extensive, most of the renovation funds were spent in constructing the kitchen and dining area, in digging out the church basement and creating a rental unit there, in building a bathroom, and in the carpentry necessary to the creation of a living space while keeping the flavor and style of the old church.

Unconventional charm and a sense of space and openness are conveyed in Ms. Koven's home—where the expression "sanctity of the hearth" is literally applied.